Dogs Are Better Than Cats

A Dog's Eye View

as told to Bob Lovka

illustrations by Ronald Lipking

BOWTIE
P R E S S

Irvine, California

Ruth Strother, project manager
Nick Clemente, special consultant
Amy Fox, editor
Liza Samala / Michael Vincent Capozzi, designers
Suzy Gehrls, production manager

Library of Congress Cataloging-in-Publication Data
Lovka, Bob, date.
  Dogs are better than cats : a dog's eye view / as told to Bob Lovka ; illustrations by Ronald Lipking.
     p. cm.
Includes index.
  ISBN 1-889540-61-7 (paperback : alk. paper)
  1. Dogs—Humor. 2. Cats—Humor. I. Title.
  PN6231.D68 L68 2001
  636.7'002'07--dc21
                                    2001002054

BowTie™ Press
3 Burroughs, Irvine, California 92618

Printed and Bound in Singapore
First Printing August 2001
10 9 8 7 6 5 4 3 2 1

A Preface of Sorts

Step into the kingdom of our furry friends and confront the timeless, all-consuming topic that rages into this millennium from past millennia on its way toward future millennia—the hotly debated Question of who's better, cats or dogs?

Now you're talking about something that goes on forever!

The Question causes heated debate in my household, where my dog, Foon, and my cat, Sonny, (both noted authors and scholars in the world of canine-feline studies) hiss, bite, scratch, shriek, bark, chase, and battle over the Answer.

Obviously, there are two schools of thought.

Using logic, metaphors, and statistics she made up, Foon has herein placed before you the case for canine superiority. The Answer, as it were, to the Great Question. By astutely observing the world of cats and dogs, and comparing the way they relate toward humans, Foon presents a concise, compelling argument for the dog side of the equation.

By defining dogs and cats in this new light, Foon hopes to lay to rest the controversy that has plagued humankind and animalkind since the beginning of time, allowing dogs to ascend to the status they so richly deserve (in Foon's opinion), that of the title, Greatest Creatures on the Planet. Dog lovers will agree.

Who's truly best? Ultimately, you will have to decide. The case is herein presented as to what dogs really are as compared to what cats really are (at least from a dog's point of view). The comments contained in this quite splendid little book are solely the words of my dog, and do not necessarily reflect the views of her roommate, me. I merely present to you a case study.

Study, think, ponder, then form your answer to the Great Question. It should be very easy to see.

—Bob Lovka
The Canine Institute of Comparative Psychology

Dogs Are

Love
A hello kiss
Noses in your lap
The peaches
Wise
Warm hearts
Richard Gere

Cats Are

Like
A final kiss-off
Noses in your business
The razzberries
Wiseacres
Cold feet
Richard Simmons

And everyone knows that
Dogs say "okay!"
Cats ask "what for?"

Dogs are lasting friends.

Cats are long gone.

And Dogs Are:

Loyal and Trustworthy!

Let's be honest. In a pinch, there's no comparison between dogs and cats. Who would you rather have driving you to the hospital in an emergency—a cat, who never has enough time, or a dog, who will make the time or even bark down an ambulance if necessary? At best, a cat will give you the phone number of a chauffeur; dogs are hands-on.

Helpful and Caring!

There is no way a cat will do your homework

for you. A dog definitely will! He will probably get it wrong, and might slobber on the papers a bit, but a dog will try! Do you know what you'll get from a cat? "Sorry, that's not my area."

Loving and Compassionate!

Got the flu? A dog will sit up all night with you and feed you chicken soup. A cat will go out to the movies with her girlfriends. Are we seeing a trend here?

In The Real World,

REX

Dogs Are

Solid as a Dollar

A lick on your face

Tail waggers

From everywhere

Chili dogs with the works

Pepperoni, sausage,
and double cheese

Cats Are

$3 bills

Two-faced

Tale tellers

From nowhere

Plain ol' wieners

Anchovy

Dogs are
soft suede
slippers.

Dogs Are

Burgers and Beer
Regular
Candlelight and wood
National Geographic
Down to earth
In it for the fun

Cats Are

Quiche and tea
Decaf
Neon and plastic
National Enquirer
Up to no good
In it for the money

*Cats are four-inch
high-heel patent
leather pumps.*

All you need to do to discover the natural superiority of dogs over cats is look around! You'll find: Seeing-Eye dogs, sled dogs, drug-sniffing police dogs, shepherding dogs, hunting dogs, and Frisbee-catching dogs. All of us working hard and helping to make the world a better place. As for cats, you've got cat burglars.

It's no coincidence that the entire English lan-

guage knows what it's talking about when it comes to dogs and cats. It's quite telling that cats are the beginning of every CATastrophe and CATaclysm, cloud the issues with CATaracts, and make the most awful CATerwauling and CATcalls when they're not being obnoxiously CATatonic!

CATegorically speaking, cats are the pits!

As language proves, dogs are much better than cats! Dogs are sultry, warm, and relaxed like the DOG days of summer. We can always be found being DO-Gooders, and we're something you'll always return to, like the DOG-eared pages of your favorite book or the contents of a restaurant DOGgie Bag. Dogs keep you afloat while you're DOG-paddling, and give you a DOGma to live by and a laugh with our DOGgerel poetry.

DOGgone it, dogs are the best!

AMAZINg   JOVIAL   SWEET

BEAUTIFUL   KIND   TRUE

CLEVER   LOYAL   UNPRETENTIOUS

DUTIFUL   MAGNIFICENT   VALOROUS

EXCELLENT   NOBLE   WELCOMING

FAITHFUL   OPTIMISTIC   X-TRA SPECIAL

GENEROUS   PLAYFUL   YIELDING

HELPFUL   QUICK-WITTED   and

INTELLIGENT   REGAL   ZANY

Cats are none of the above!

As for Affection,

BOWSER

Dogs cry over sentimental old movies.

Dogs are puppy love
Dogs sympathize
Dogs hug
Dogs kiss
Dogs send flowers

Cats are cat fights
Cats say, "I told you so!"
Cats shake hands
Cats give you a little peck
Cats send bills

Cats smirk and get more popcorn.

Yep, it all comes down to this:
Dogs are sincere
Cats are superficial

Dogs don't mess around with your affections. We have no one-night stands. Dogs are committed! A dog is there for you whether it's Monday afternoon or Saturday night. Whether you or your hair is having a bad day, a dog doesn't mind. Dogs are in for the long haul and are happy

to guard you and protect you in the bargain!

Try a relationship with a cat and it's a bunch of excuses, last minute cancellations, and a need for her own space. The only space a dog wants is the one right next to you. In the same space is even better.

Dogs are romance novels.

Dogs bond, leap, lick, and love! If your face isn't handy for licking, your ankle will do. Cats? If you're lucky, you might get a patronizing "mew" of recognition once in a while. As for physical contact, dogs love to be petted—a lot! Cats allow you to pet them—a little.

Dogs Are

Perpetual kids

Cats Are

Grown-ups

And while dogs give
unconditional love,
cats have to think about it!

Cats are mysteries.

Dogs are a kiss on the face.

Dogs Are

Over easy
Pursuers

Do you ever
have days when
you look like an old
dishrag and feel
about the same?
Days when even your
own clothes don't want
to be seen with you?

Cats Are

Hard-boiled
The pursued

A dog doesn't care!
Ask a dog what you
look like and he'll lick
your face and tell you
you're looking great!
Cats? They're vicious.
They'll tell you the
truth. Who needs that?

Cats are a kick in the butt.

The Affection Connection

When it comes right down to it, dogs are just around more than cats. Do you want a part-time pet? A freelancer? A fair-weather friend who may or may not be there when you walk through the door? Then by all means take up with a cat! I know some cats whose allegiance to their humans is here today, somewhere else tomorrow, and "I'll get back to you" when you call. To dogs, that's just plain bigamy! To put it simply,

dogs are marriage partners and cats are gigolos.

Do you stay out late? A dog will wait up worrying over you. And if a dog could operate a stove, he would have some warm cocoa waiting, too. A cat couldn't care less—that is if the cat is even home! Most likely the cat will stay out all night, not call, then next day tell you she was out watching over a sick friend.

Right. And Lassie was a raccoon.

Dogs Are

Gin Rummy, Poker, Bridge, and Canasta
The biggest slice
Triple-layer, double Dutch chocolate birthday cakes
Malt liquor

Dogs are Harleys.

Cats Are

Solitaire
The last little piece
Hostess Twinkies
Lite beer

Cats are scooters.

And dogs listen,
while cats ignore!

Let's Have a Talk

It's no surprise that dogs keep secrets and cats gossip. You've heard of the term catty? Well?

Dogs listen to you even when you have nothing to say, are sympathetic when you need a paw and a pal, and always keep your secrets untold. As for your "friend" the cat, within minutes of telling little Fluffy anything, the whole world knows! Cats are faster than the Internet in spreading information—and rumors. And, worse, cats use information against you! Tell a cat something important then notice how she

reacts—she's either total "who-cares" bore-
dom or she gives that coy, half-interested look
that means, "I'm taping this."
Beware. Cats
file away
information
to use
luter.

Dogs Are

Mashed potatoes and gravy
The Texas Rangers
Marines
Steak
Galaxies
Apples
Hockey
Common folk
Top dogs
Smile

*Dogs are your
best friend.*

Cats Are

Vichyssoise soup
The Lone Ranger
Coast Guard reserves
Quiche
Spaced out
Sour grapes
Golf
Haughty
Scaredy cats
Smirk

And who's more
playful and fun?
It's not even close!

Dogs are ready, willing, and able to have fun with you. Want to throw a ball around? Toss a Frisbee? Wrestle? Play hide-and-seek? *Name it* and a dog will join in! Ask a cat to catch a Frisbee, and all you'll get is a look that says, "You must be joking."

Cats are your worst nightmare.

Dogs are Hawaiian shirts and polka dots.

Cats are too stuffy to play with you. It's not proper. It's undignified. As comedians, cats are satire, dogs are slapstick! Yes, a cat will leap, pounce, roll, or tear around like a maniac, but not with you. Believe me, cats are snobs! They have a definite cattitude and a huge superiority complex. A dog is down to earth. A dog is a common Joe. At most, we dogs might think of ourselves as human. Cats think they're gods.

Dogs Are

Alert

Mom 'n' pop shops

Egg cremes

Wholesale

The open road and wind
in your hair

Cats Are

Aloof

Multinational conglomerates

Eggs Benedict

Retail

Chauffeur-driven limos with
the windows blacked out

And dogs splash in puddles
as they play in the rain.
Cats—(are you kidding?).

*Cats are three-piece
suits and pinstripes.*

By all accounts, dogs are reliable, loyal, and courageous. We're here to help out! Dogs have a sense of duty, can follow instructions and commands, and always have your best interest in mind. And even an ordinary mutt can be a hero!

A dog will guard your property and protect your person. Dogs come to your rescue. Try counting on that with a cat! Even the movies and television pay homage to this characteristic of dogs. Remember Lassie and Ol' Yeller and

Tramp? Wouldn't you feel safe with 101 dalmatians?

What's in a Name? Plenty!

Do you really believe that some little hairball named Froo-Froo is going to dig you out of a snowbank? Nope! That's a job for Bernard, as in Saint Bernard. Think a burglar will run away from Fluffy's ferocious meow? Right. Get Spike or Butkus or Rocky into the act, and the burglar's gone!

Sometimes you can tell a book by its cover—or name.

Cats are Missy and Purr-Purr and Snowball and Foofie. Dogs are Rex and Bear and Shane and Rambo. Who are you going to call when the chips are down?

And when was the last time you saw Princess Frisky on the job at a fire station? By any name, a dog will protect and serve. It's just a part of who we are.

Dogs go for walks.

Certainly You've Noticed That

BELLA

Dogs
Ask
Laugh

Cats
Demand
Smirk

...all-in-all proving
dogs are much more
appreciative than cats!

Cats must be chauffeured.

Come home loaded down with grocery bags or shopping packages, and a dog is ecstatic: "Is there anything, any little crumb at all, for me? Wow! thank-you, thank-you, thank-you for that forty-nine cent pepperoni stick! Yeah!"

A cat, on the other paw, assumes that if anybody walks through her door loaded down with parcels, boxes, and grocery bags it must be tribute, hom-

age, and some gifts (which cats always feel they deserve). You'll get a survey of the scene, a quick sniff, a little rummaging around, and a look twenty seconds later that says, "Is that all?" Arrogance? Thy name is cat! If cats were dogs people would be forced to use 24k gold pooper scoopers.

And dogs let you dress them up for holidays.

Cats? Not a chance!

The Differences Between Dogs and Cats

Dogs...

Take an overnight bag
Lick you to love you
Believe in you
Take action
Keep bank accounts

*Dogs play
with your feet.*

Cats...

Pack everything but the kitchen sink

Lick you to taste you

Have their doubts

Take readings and calculations

Speculate in whole-life
insurance, buy options,
and swap tech stocks

And just by watching us
you can tell—dogs dream,
cats plot! Emotionally and
geographically speaking, dogs
and cats are New York and Los Angeles.

**Cats get
underfoot.**

It was a cat who first rolled her eyes and coined the L.A. catchword *Whatever*. In fact, if you love L.A., you'll identify with cats—cats and people from L.A. are indifferent, blase, laid-back (read "brain dead"), and impermanent, and both profess the same philosophy: "Hey, like

it's here today, gone tomorrow. Whatever...."
Carrying on a meaningful conversation with a
cat is like conversing with a mushroom, except
the mushroom won't walk away in the middle of
your sentence. A meaningful L.A./cat conversation goes, "Yeah...Uh-huh. Like, yeah.")

Dogs, on the other paw, are New York: emotional, articulate (everybody has something to say, and usually it's in more than one syllable), and like people from New York, dogs are totally involved with you! Dogs get happy when you're happy, act frantic when you're in a panic, and we chase our tails in support of you when you're running around in circles. The most emotional

support a cat will share with you is snoring. You can get more interaction from a pet mummy, although it might be just as "laid-back."

Dogs are interactive. When the word *interpassive* is invented, it will be applied first to cats.

I ask you, is this a suitable companion for a reasonably conscious human being?

REBEL

Dogs Are

Emotional
Supportive
Empathetic
Selfless

Dogs are friendly.

Cats Are

Analytical
Controlling
Pathetic
Selfish

And while dogs volunteer, cats go into salary negotiations.

Cats are downright diabolical! They will agree to ANYTHING, then turn around and do whatever they want. Cats make great politicians. Dogs? They're working stiffs.

Cats are standoffish.

The Understanding Dog vs. the Cat Who Needs a Viable Explanation

A dog is understanding. If you get home late and dinnertime was three hours ago, a dog doesn't mind. Traffic? Late meeting at work? Someone a little interesting at the martini bar?

No sweat! You do have a life and your best friend supports that. We're just glad you come back! (Run that can opener when you get a chance, please.)

Ever come home late on a cat? It's not a pretty sight. First there's the guilt-tinged "Where were mewww?" Then the stare that says, "You know I'm a creature of habit, my diet is important, now you're upsetting my biological clock and what was soooo important anyway?" I have seen a caretaker forced to produce a note from the boss explaining why said caretaker was kept late. And the cat was still miffed!

Cats demand explanations but treat them as

excuses. ("You had a previous obligation and should have been here.") And, boy do cats get even for excuses! Little Purr-Purr wouldn't eat for three days after the late dinner episode. (Actually, she was sneaking food on the side but her caretakers will never know that.) Since then her caretaker has quit the job and takes in laundry to support them both from home—and never misses dinnertime.

Want a housemate and a life?
Get a dog!

Dogs Are

Oscar Madison
Sunday afternoon football
Steamboats
Potato salad
Borrowers
Gyms
Bench presses,
squats, and curls
Passionate
Computer hardware

Dogs are bourbon
and branch water.

Cats Are

Felix Unger

Weekday afternoon soaps

Canoes

Potato leek soup

Lenders

Spas

Treadmills, stretches,
and aerobics

Cool

Computer software

Cats are
wine spritzers.

And one of the nicest things
dogs are is communicative...

...Granted, a dog's communication to you is mostly in the form of: "Can I sit there?" "How about going for a walk!" and, "You sure you can eat ALL that?" but it's honest and easily understood. With cats you're never sure of what you think you might have heard, or what the cat is really communicating. They're sneaky that way, and they give you the same dumb stare making you read into it whatever you might. The cat's thinking is, "If I'm noncommittal, I may get an

apology, a toy, more food, or some leverage in future dealings. I'll let them worry about it!"

Humans feel absolutely terrible when they can't figure out what a pet is saying. Dogs try to help you out of this anxiety. Cats encourage it. It gives them more bargaining power.

Cats seldom tell you anything completely. They like to feel superior by giving you only a bit of information or a partial communication. It's always been that way.

It's So Easy to See That...

BEAR

Dogs...

Rock
Walk
Advance
Cooperate
Discuss

Dogs trot.

Cats...

Roll
Take cabs
Withdraw
Oppose
Chat

Cats slink.

Vacation: With a Dog or with a Cat?

On vacation, dogs are part of the fun! At the beach we're the first ones in the water, jumping onto waves, bounding into surf, discovering great kelp and old sticks, and bringing you seaweed. In the mountains, we love to hike. Dogs sniff out the tallest trees and even help you with your fishing. Dogs are partners and pals in the

great outdoors, and what's a campfire song without canine accompaniment! Take a cat anywhere and she'll end up UP a tree instead of sniffing around it.

   Humans take vacations with their dogs. They take vacations away from their cats.

Dogs Are

Sunny days
Oceans
Accepting
Definitely
Circles
Catchers
Sunbeams
Oaks
Beards
Crumb cakes
Come what may

Dogs are cowboy boots.

Cats Are

Rainy days
Ponds
Judgmental
Probably
Zigzags
Chasers
Moonbeams
Willows
Whiskers
Crumbs
Schedules and timetables

Cats are bunny slippers.

Dogs Are There for You!

You can't get empathy or sympathy from a cat.

Cats are too busy and too wrapped up in themselves to give you the support you need when problems and pains arise. Let's say you smack your finger in a door and let out a scream. A dog is right there, running around, sniffing everything, looking up at you frantically asking, "WHA' HAPPENED! WHATDOYOUNEED!

WHO DID IT? TELL ME! TELL ME! I'LL GET 'EM FOR YOU!"

Then, as you run cold water over your damaged digit and pack it in some ice, Fido or Foon or Rex is beside you ("YOU HURT, I HURT; LEMME KISS THE BOO-BOO!"), waiting to hear the whole story. It's important to him! ("TELL ME HOW IT HAPPENED! WANT ME TO BITE THE DOOR? ANYTHING! LEMME HELP!")

A cat—unless your painful scream hasn't awakened her from another nap, or she isn't totally engrossed (for 10 seconds) with some stupid stuffed mouse, will take one look at you that says, "That was stupid, wasn't it?" and schedule you for a talk later on the proper technique of opening and closing doors. Then, since you so seem to be so wrapped up in this "door thing" anyway, the cat will tell you to open the miserable door and let her out! For all the cat

really cares, your finger could be lying on the floor. (She'd step over it on her way out.) Silly you! Your fingers and the door exist for only one purpose—to let the cat come in and go out. If you catch a finger in the door, you're not doing your job properly—and that merits correction, not concern over your welfare. Cats never support or comfort, they control. Need a little T-bone and sympathy? You know who will be there.

Dogs are jazz,
bebop, and
swing.

Dogs Are

Down home
Confederate
Casual
"Hip-hip-hooray!!"
Interested
Accidental
Involved
Accepting
Wacko
Players

Cats are quadrilles,
minuets, and
standing.

Cats Are

Downtown
Union
Formal
"Oh, how nice for you."
Indifferent
Intentional
Aloof
Finicky
Psycho
Watchers

And dogs are willing to learn,
while cats think they
know better!

SHANE

Dogs rescue
Dogs respond
Dogs protect
Dogs express feelings
Dogs fetch for you!

Dogs walk with you.

Cats don't get involved

Cats ignore

Cats feel it's none of their concern

Cats withhold judgment

Cats hire others to do that!

And to set the record straight:
dogs clean, cats preen.

Cats walk on you.

Let's Talk About This
Tidiness Business

Cats have the reputation for being soooo clean and soooo neat in comparison to dogs, and it's all soooo untrue!

The way a cat gets "clean" is by leaving her dirty cat hair all over your clothes—and carpets and bed and ceiling. Somehow even a black cat can leave white hair on a black suit or dress, and no matter how meticulous a cat's caretaker is, there will always be some cat hair somewhere on every possession the caretaker

owns. Cats are not clean (*gato non cleano* in many parts of the world); they just sneak around and drop off their dirty laundry for humans to deal with!

Dogs are honest. When a dog is dirty, you know it. We'll take a bath, shake off the soap and water, and we're none the worse for the experience. You won't find six hundred tiny hairs in your soup or your shirt pocket later on.

Yes, some of us do shed, but at least we don't climb up into your clothes closet to find your Gucci dress or Armani suit to do it on. Dogs try to shed in clumps and leave the hair somewhere that won't cause you consternation. No cat is that thoughtful. The closest thing you'll get to any kind of cat consideration is a hairball in your best shoes. Dogs are considerate (and clean). Cats simply don't care.

Dogs are athletic.

Dogs Are

Humble
Exact
Literal
Even-tempered
Verbal

Cats Are

Presumptuous
Approximate
Figurative
Temperamental
Mental

Cats are aesthetic.

And while dogs are ready to go anywhere, cats are asking for details about the trip!

Dogs are along for the ride, cats are going their own way.

Dogs are much more like humans than cats!

Dogs share many of the nicest qualities of people. Dogs apologize for mistakes and wrong-doings. Cats never feel the need. And when a human makes a mistake, a dog understands. Cats? No way! Cats keep score of your faults

and mistakes, using them against you whenever you try to criticize them! It's said that "To err is human," but the second half of that saying is "but to forgive is not feline." Screw up with a cat and she'll never let you forget it. Also, dogs are willing to improve ourselves (cats believe they're already perfect!) and will even go to obedience school if you insist. The only school a cat is likely to attend is a school for anarchy.

   Dogs are easy on people. We fess up to our faults and accept responsibility. Dogs are sincere and even show remorse. Cats maintain their innocence, acting as if whatever they did never even happened. That's because dogs have a conscience; cats have conviction. Self-centered conviction. Cats shift the blame—most times to an innocent dog—or give a blank stare that says, "I haven't the foggiest idea of what you're talking about." And they don't! Cats are like lawyers that way. It's all semantics:

Human: Yikes! Who was on the bed sleeping on my new pillow?

Cat: Define the terms *bed* and *pillow*, and clarify what constitutes a new pillow.

Human: Come on. Who was on the bed?

Cat: The house in question contains three bedrooms comprised of four beds total. To which bed are you referring?

On and on it goes, and you can bet that down the line the dog will get blamed. Yet dogs and people are a perfect match. It's no coincidence that dogs (and people) have toenails. Cats have claws. And no human feels threatened by bad luck when a black dog crosses his or her path. It's obvious: dogs fit in. Cats intrude.

And While...

BUFFY

Dogs get enthused
Dogs wait by the door
Dogs enjoy
Dogs hope
Dogs trust
Dogs bring you slippers
Dogs take walks in
the rain with you

Dogs are watchful.

Cats couldn't care less
Cats wait on top of the bed
Cats tolerate
Cats expect
Cats suspect
Cats bring you headaches
Cats stay inside (because
in the rain, dogs frolic
and cats freak!)

Cats just stare.

What It All Comes Down to Is

Dogs are everything you could hope for in a pal, a pet, and a family member! We're here being your best friends, and we're "there," too, when the people world gets to be a bit much.

Dogs are a little bit of everything good, and are the bearers of knock-down, lick-in-the-face, unconditional love delivered direct with no postage due from you. What we dogs feel it all comes down to is that a dog's heart is out in the open, a cat's heart is locked away.